The Interaction
of the Soul and Body

The Interaction
of the Soul and Body

from the Latin of
Emanuel Swedenborg

The Swedenborg Society
20-21 Bloomsbury Way
London, WC1A 2TH

2001

NOTE

The present version of *De Commercio Animae et Corporis*,
originally published in London, in 1769, is a reprint of the
1996 edition. The 1996 version is based upon the edition issued by the
Swedenborg Society in 1844, revised in 1897 and again in 1925, and
re-issued in 1947 under the title *The Intercourse of the Soul and the
Body*. An index has been added to the current edition and the title has
been shortened to *The Interaction of the Soul and Body*.

The small numerals on the outer margins indicate the
subdivisions of the longer paragraphs made by the Rev J F Potts, BA,
and introduced by him into his *Concordance to the Theological
Writings of Emanuel Swedenborg*.

Published by:
The Swedenborg Society
Swedenborg House
20-21 Bloomsbury Way
London WC1A 2TH

© The Swedenborg Society

Book Design: Stephen McNeilly
Design Consultant: Mikaela Dyhlén

Typeset at Swedenborg House.
Printed and bound in Great Britain
at Biddles.

ISBN 0 85448 129 x
British Library Cataloguing in Publication Data.
A Catalogue record for this book is available
from the British Library.

Introduction

❧❧❧❧❧❧❧❧❧❧❧❧❧❧❧❧❧❧❧

Mankind has always sought to understand how ideas can be gained by the mind through the body's experience, and also how the soul enters the mind and forms ideas and controls the body's purpose. This little work was written by Swedenborg late in his life, and was framed to show his thought on these matters and to comment on philosophical ideas known in his day. Often he writes here to show the fallacy in philosophical reasoning, and sounds like the philosopher he was before he began his work of revelation; but he also speaks frankly about what he has seen in the spiritual world, and makes those revelations part of his argument. When he deals with the same subject in *Arcana Caelestia* volume 8, in the sections at the end of Genesis chapters 46 to 50, he begins immediately from what has been revealed to him, and does not touch on the philosophical theories with which he begins here. There is no difference in the message, but it is clear that this little work is directed to those who might know the philosophy and wish to set it in a correct light.

In *De Commercio*, he states his view against the solutions which have been suggested by philosophers. Some of these, ranging from Plato through to Berkeley, have regarded the ideas in the soul as being the reality inflowing into the body and causing all activity of the mind. A similar approach showed in

Descartes' efforts to revive philosophy in the seventeenth century. He reasoned that one might doubt everything, but must accept that this meant there was a doubter, a thinker. 'I think, therefore I am'. Since this thinker has an idea of God, God must exist to cause such an idea, for it is not possible to invent something greater than one is. Along these lines, in an age of reason, Descartes sought to establish the mind and God in preference to relying on the body and its senses. Later, Kant was to argue a similar primacy in different guise. On the other hand, others have asserted that it is the body which brings about the activity of the mind, so that its ideas are generated from the body. Although it was not the view of Aristotle, this view gained strength from his idea that the forms of ideas and matter are not separate spheres but cohere in one substance. This caused a confused tendency among the medieval Schoolmen and their successors to emphasise matter and its influence entering through the body. Here nominalism became dominant, the concept that any general idea or principle is only a name and has no real existence as do the particulars existing in experience. All activity of the mind was seen as inflowing from the body's experience. This view reached its apotheosis in the teaching of complete scepticism by David Hume (who was Swedenborg's contemporary); and it finds its completeness in modern empiricism, and in materialistic views which see all the mind's characteristics as mere epiphenomena of the physical world. The only other philosophical solution to the interaction of the soul and the body is the one associated with Leibnitz. This arose from the difficulty of seeing how activity in the soul could affect matter and vice versa, which he solved by the assumption that there was no such interaction. God had ordained that the two followed parallel courses. Bodily and mental activity have no causal relationship, but exist parallel to each other in a "pre-established harmony".

Such a brief summary can only call to mind the theories involved, and will perhaps convey little to someone not versed in philosophy, but the basic problem under discussion is clear enough and is clearly stated in *De Commercio*. Either the mind works simply from impressions which enter through the body, or there is an influx within from a soul which causes the mind's activity in the body, or the mind's activity runs parallel to the body's activity without any inter-action at all.

The ideas Swedenborg had already published in earlier works can help us to grasp the background to what he says here; and also perhaps to grasp the limitation of the kinds of philosophy he discusses and compares to his own vision. In *The Divine Love and Wisdom* he made clear that the only thing which exists in itself is life, and this we call God. The nature of that life is love. Love is a word which we use in many human relationships, and he is careful to give a specific definition of this divine love: it seeks to give what is its own to another as if it were that other's own. Two things result from this. Life that is God must create others to fulfil its love; and those others must be free to choose whether they accept God's giving kind of love, or whether they assume they have life to use for themselves. In other words, they must be able to accept that life in free-dom as their own. Fulfilment of this means that God will create an increasing number of individual souls to receive His love, and He will set them in such an environment that they are free to choose to accept that love or not. The nature of creation results from this activity of divine love. In contrast to this, it must be realised that the interest of the philosophers discussed is chiefly in the realm of thought, and the idea of love as the prime factor in the human mind hardly occurs, still less any thought of the nature of God's love creating.

All of creation is to set men and women in a situation where they can receive life apparently as their own. To do this, each must have a separate soul into which life is gifted, and then this must be able to act into a mind and body set in an environment that is not part of God, but which is maintained by His life and set, as it were, distinctly "over against" it. If each individual is to be free to choose, the basis of this environment must be fixed so that it does not react to the way the individual chooses to use life. Hence the nature of the physical world and the body living in it. These are being created continually by God for man's use, but it is essential that we are not aware of this as we live in them. In them, God's creative activity comes to rest in a fixed realm which provides a reactive plane to the soul within. Between the two develops the activity which is the mind of man, active on many levels. Here is the solution to the puzzle presented by our ability to comprehend and understand the world around us by using our senses. The same life which creates the external world is alive in our soul, and puts together the external stimuli of light waves and physical forces into something we see and feel, and which we can then appreciate, value and use and so direct our actions. The whole of the mind's activity depends on the soul inflowing and making intelligible the reactive plane of the body in its environment. The activity of that mind is not a mere pursuit of knowledge but the choice of a life active from God's kind of love. This is the basis of Swedenborg's ideas on the soul and the body and the influx between them.

In all the approach from philosophy, the aspect of thought and reason is dominant, and little or no consideration is given to the driving force of love which is the heart of Swedenborg's approach. Later, in the nineteenth century, Schopenhauer claimed to have originated the idea of the will as the prime mover in man, but his thought brought about little development. This is understandable, for there is no way the human mind can conceive ideas of God and His nature. Clearly God must reveal them. In the treatment in *De Commercio*, Swedenborg uses without any apology such ideas revealed to him, but he tries to show how they illuminate the conclusions of philosophical thought.

In his discussion he treats of the two realms of the soul and the body in terms of two 'suns': one of which is spiritual and provides the soul and its activity, and the other of which is material and maintains the physical body and its surroundings. Care is needed in following his argument here. He speaks of 'a sun' of the physical world as being the source of its existence and subsistence. Yet his Writings show him well aware that there are many suns in our galaxy and, indeed, other galaxies than our own. He is speaking in terms of what appears to us in this world. There we see the sun as the centre and origin of planets and the maintainer of heat and light which bring about all the activities of worldly things. For our experience, this is the sun of our natural sphere, whatever might appear to one on a planet around a star in another galaxy. Our sun is seen as the supplier of natural heat and light and the consequent activity.

He contrasts this with the 'sun' of the spiritual world.   In itself, this will be the activity of the love of God flowing into the soul of each individual. He refers to it as a sun because that is how it appears in the spiritual world to men and women there. Its reality is the activity of the love of God, which is the life in their souls, but its real appearance to them is as a sun. Thus in these two 'suns', he can contrast the activity of the body in this world, and the activity of the soul from the Divine which gives it life.

This book constantly recalls the thought of philosophers from their reason, and the introduction into it of ideas revealed to Swedenborg in the spiritual world seems at first anomalous. Yet this really makes the principal point, namely, that the human mind cannot gain knowledge of God and His purposes, nor of the soul and its activity in the body, but must have it revealed. Once those ideas are known, they can be used to illuminate and correct thought which depended solely on the exercise of human reason; and also can provide a detailed under-standing of the way human minds are meant to work. It is therefore fitting that Swedenborg finishes his book with two of his experiences in the spiritual world. One judges between the attitudes of philosophers about the interaction of the soul and the body in the figures of Descartes for influx from the soul, the Schoolmen relying in a shadowy way on Aristotle for influx from the body, and Leibnitz for his pre-established harmony of soul and body. The other experi-ence shows Swedenborg's own development from a natural philosopher to one who reveals and uses spiritual truths, for without those nothing can really be known.

Paul V Vickers

Contents

‹›

Contents

Contents

___

___

The Interaction
of the Soul and Body

1. There are three opinions and traditions, which are hypotheses, concerning the Interaction of the Soul and Body, or the operation of the one upon the other, and of the one together with the other: the first is called Physical Influx, the second Spiritual Influx, and the third Pre-established Harmony.

The *first*, which is called *physical influx*, arises from the appearances of the senses, and the fallacies thence derived. For it appears as if the objects of sight, which affect the eyes, flow into the thought and produce it; in like manner speech, which affects the ears, appears to flow into the mind, and to produce ideas there; and it is similar with respect to the senses of smell, taste, and touch. Since the organs of these senses first receive the impressions that flow into them from the world, and the mind appears to think, and also to will, according as these organs are affected, therefore, the ancient philosophers and Schoolmen believed that influx was derived from them into the soul, and hence adopted the hypothesis of Physical or Natural Influx.

---

2   The *second* hypothesis, which is called *spiritual*, and by some *occasional influx,* originates in order and its laws. For the soul is a spiritual substance, and therefore purer, prior, and interior; but the body is material, and therefore grosser, posterior, and exterior; and it is according to order that the purer should flow into the grosser, the prior into the posterior, and the interior into the exterior, thus what is spiritual into what is material, and not the contrary. Consequently, it is according to order for the thinking mind to flow into the sight according to the state induced on the eyes by the objects before them, which state that mind also disposes at its pleasure; and likewise for the perceptive mind to flow into the hearing, according to the state induced upon the ears by speech.

3   The *third* hypothesis, which is called *pre-established harmony*, arises from the appearances and fallacies of the reasoning faculty; since the mind, in the very act of operating, acts together with and at the same time as the body. Still, every operation is first successive and afterwards simultaneous, and successive operation is Influx, and simultaneous operation is Harmony; as, for instance, when the mind thinks and afterwards speaks, or when it wills and afterwards acts: hence it is a fallacy of the reasoning faculty to establish that which is simultaneous, and to exclude that which is successive.

No fourth opinion concerning the Interaction of the Soul and the Body can be framed in addition to these three; for either the soul must operate upon the body, or the body upon the soul, or both uninterruptedly at the same time.

2. Since Spiritual Influx, as we have said, originates in order and its laws, it has been acknowledged and received by the wise in the learned world in preference to the other two opinions. Everything which originates in order is truth, and truth, in virtue of its own inherent light, manifests itself even in the shade of the reasoning faculty in which hypotheses reside. As, however, there are three things which involve this hypothesis in shade—ignorance as to what the soul is, ignorance as to what is spiritual, and ignorance respecting the nature of influx—these three things must first be explained before the rational faculty

can see the truth itself. For hypothetical truth is not truth itself, but a conjecture of the truth. It is like a picture on a wall seen at night by the light of the stars, to which the mind assigns a form varying according to its fancy; but which appears different after daybreak, when the light of the sun shines upon it, and not only reveals and presents to view its general features, but also each of its parts. So, from the shade of truth in which this hypothesis resides, is produced the open truth, when it is known what and of what nature is that which is spiritual respectively to that which is natural; as also what and of what nature is the human soul, and what the nature of the influx into it, and through it into the perceptive and thinking mind, and from this into the body.

But these subjects can be explained by no one, unless it has been granted him by the Lord to be consociated with angels in the spiritual world and at the same time with men in the natural world; and because this has been granted to me, I have been enabled to describe what and of what nature they both are. This has been done in the work on *Conjugial Love*: concerning what is *spiritual*, in the memorable relation, nos. 326-329; concerning the *human soul*, no. 315; and concerning *influx*, no. 380, and still more fully at nos. 415-422.* Who does not know, or may not know, that the good of love and the truth of faith flow in from God into man, and that they flow into his soul, and are felt in his mind; and that they flow forth from his thought into his speech, and from his will into his actions?

That Spiritual Influx is thence, and also its origin and derivation, shall be shown in the following order:

I *There are two worlds: the spiritual world, inhabited by spirits and angels, and the natural world, inhabited by men.*

II *The spiritual world first existed and continually subsists from its own sun; and the natural world from its own sun.*

———

* The same articles may be found in *The True Christian Religion*, at nos. 280, 697, 35, 77 and 12.

——

III *The sun of the spiritual world is pure love from Jehovah God, who is in the midst of it.*

IV *From that sun proceed heat and light; the heat proceeding from it is in its essence love, and the light from it is in its essence wisdom.*

V *Both that heat and that light flow into man: the heat into his will, where it produces the good of love; and the light into his understanding, where it produces the truth of wisdom.*

VI *Those two, heat and light, or love and wisdom, flow conjointly from God into the soul of man; and through this into his mind, its affections and thoughts; and from these into the senses, speech, and actions of the body.*

VII *The sun of the natural world is pure fire; and the world of nature first existed and continually subsists by means of this sun.*

VIII *Therefore everything which proceeds from this sun, regarded in itself, is dead.*

IX *That which is spiritual clothes itself with that which is natural, as a man clothes himself with a garment.*

X *Spiritual things thus clothed in a man enable him to live as a rational and moral man, thus as a spiritually natural man.*

XI *The reception of that influx is according to the state of love and wisdom with man.*

XII *The understanding in man can be raised into the light, that is, into the wisdom, in which are the angels of heaven, according to the cultivation of his reason; and his will can be raised, in like manner, into heat, that is, into love, according to the deeds of his life; but the love of the will is not raised, except so far as the man wills and does those things which the wisdom of the understanding teaches.*

XIII *It is altogether otherwise with beasts.*

XIV *There are three degrees in the spiritual world, and three degrees in the natural world, according to which all influx takes place.*

XV *Ends are in the first degree, causes in the second, and effects in the third.*

XVI *Hence is evident the nature of spiritual influx from its origin to its effects.*

Each of these propositions shall now be briefly illustrated.

—

There are two worlds:
the spiritual world, inhabited by spirits and angels, and the natural world, inhabited by men

3. **T**hat there is a spiritual world inhabited by spirits and angels distinct from the natural world inhabited by men, has hitherto been deeply hidden, even in the Christian world, because no angel has descended and taught it by word of mouth, nor has any man ascended and seen it. Lest, therefore, from ignorance of that world, and the uncertain faith respecting heaven and hell thence resulting, man should be so far infatuated as to become an atheistic materialist, it has pleased the Lord to open the sight of my spirit, and to raise it into heaven and let it down into hell, and to exhibit to my view the nature of both.

It has thus been made evident to me that there are two worlds, distinct from each other; one, in which all things are spiritual, whence it is called the spiritual world; and the other, in which all things are natural, whence it is called the natural world: and also that spirits and angels live in their own world, and men in theirs; and further, that every man passes by death from his world into the other, and lives in it to eternity. In order that Influx, which is the subject of this little work, may be unfolded from its beginning, it is necessary that some information respecting both these worlds should be provided; for the spiritual world flows into the natural world, and actuates it in all its parts, with both men and beasts, and also constitutes the vegetative principle in trees and herbs.

2

The spiritual world first existed and continually subsists from its own sun; and the natural world from its own sun

4. That there is one sun of the spiritual world and another of the natural world is because those worlds are altogether distinct from each other, and a world derives its origin from a sun. For a world in which all things are spiritual cannot originate from a sun, all the products of which are natural, since thus there would be physical influx, which, however, is contrary to order. That the world came into existence from the sun, and not the sun from the world, is evident from the consequence of the fact that the world, as to all things belonging to it, in general and in particular, subsists by means of the sun; and subsistence proves existence, hence it is said that subsistence is perpetual existence: thus it is evident that if the sun were removed its world would fall into chaos, and this chaos into nothing.

2   That in the spiritual world there is a sun different from that in the natural world I am able to testify, for I have seen it: in appearance it is fiery, like our sun, of nearly the same magnitude, and at a distance from the angels as our sun is from men. It does not rise or set, however, but stands immovable in a middle altitude between the zenith and the horizon, whence the angels enjoy perpetual light and perpetual spring.

3   A man given to reasoning, who knows nothing concerning the sun of the spiritual world, easily becomes insane in his idea of the creation of the universe.

When he deeply considers it, he perceives no otherwise than that it is from nature; and because the origin of nature is the sun, that it is from its sun as a creator. Moreover, no one can have a perception of spiritual influx, unless he also knows its origin: for all influx proceeds from a sun; spiritual influx from its sun, and natural influx from its sun. The internal sight of a man, which is the sight of his mind, receives influx from the spiritual sun; but the external sight, which is that of the body, receives influx from the natural sun, and in operation they unite, just as the soul does with the body.

Hence it is evident into what blindness, darkness, and stupidity those may   4
fall who know nothing of the spiritual world and its sun; into *blindness,* because the mind, depending solely upon the sight of the eye, becomes in its reasonings like a bat, which flies by night in a wandering course, and some-times into linen clothes which may be hanging up; into *darkness,* because the sight of the mind, when the sight of the eye is flowing into it from within, is deprived of all spiritual light [*lumen*], and becomes like that of an owl; into *stupidity,* because the man still thinks, but from natural things about spiritual, and not the other way round; consequently, idiotically, foolishly, and insanely.

—III—

The sun of the spiritual world is pure love
from Jehovah God, who is in the midst of it

⊱⊰⊱⊰⊱⊰⊱⊰⊱⊰⊱⊰⊱⊰⊱⊰⊱⊰⊱⊰⊱⊰⊱⊰

5.   Spiritual things cannot proceed from any other source than from love, nor love from any other source than from Jehovah God, who is love itself: hence the sun of the spiritual world, from which, as from their fountain, all spiritual things stream forth, is pure love proceeding from Jehovah God, who is in the midst of it. That sun itself is not God, but is from God: it is the nearest sphere around Him from Himself. By means of this sun the universe was created by Jehovah God; by which are meant all worlds considered as one whole, which are as many as the stars in the expanse of our heaven.

2   Creation was effected by means of that sun, which is pure love, thus by Jehovah God, because love is the very Being [*esse*] of life, and wisdom is the Manifestation [*existere*] of life from thence, and all things were created from love by means of wisdom. This is understood by these words in John: *"The Word was with God, and God was the Word. All things were made by Him, and without Him was not anything made that was made: and the world was made by Him"* (1:1,3,10). The Word there is the Divine Truth, thus likewise the Divine Wisdom; therefore, also, the Word is there called (ver. 9) the light which enlightens every man, in like manner as does the Divine Wisdom by means of the Divine Truth.

———

Those who deduce the origin of worlds from any other source than from the   3
Divine Love by means of the Divine Wisdom are deluded like those mentally
afflicted, who see spectres as men, phantoms as luminous objects, and imagi-
nary beings as real figures. For the created universe is a coherent work, from
love by means of wisdom: this you will see, if you are able to view the connec-
tion of things in order, from first principles to ultimates.

As God is one, so also the spiritual sun is one; for extension of space is not   4
predicable of spiritual things, which are its derivations: and essence and existence, which are without space, are everywhere in spaces without space; thus the
Divine Love is everywhere from the beginning of the universe to all its bounda-
ries. That the Divine fills all things, and by such infilling preserves them in the
state in which they were created, the rational faculty sees remotely: and it sees it
more nearly, in proportion as it has a knowledge of the nature of love as it is in
itself; of its conjunction with wisdom that ends may be perceived, of its influx
into wisdom that causes may be exhibited, and of its operation by means of
wisdom that effects may be produced.

**From that sun proceed heat and light;
the heat proceeding from it is in its essence love,
and the light from it is in its essence wisdom**

≈≈≈≈≈≈≈≈≈≈≈≈≈≈≈≈≈≈≈≈≈

6.   It is well known that in the Word, and thence in the common language of preachers, the Divine Love is expressed by fire; as when prayer is offered that heavenly fire may fill the heart, and kindle holy desires to worship God: the reason is that fire corresponds to love, and thence signifies it. Hence it is that Jehovah God appeared before Moses as a fire in the bush, and in like manner before the children of Israel on Mount Sinai; and that it was commanded for fire to be kept perpetually upon the altar, and for the lights of the lamp-stand in the tabernacle to be lighted every evening: these commands were given because fire signified love.

2   That such fire has heat proceeding from it appears plainly from the effects of love: thus a man is set on fire, grows warm, and becomes inflamed, as his love is exalted into zeal, or into the glow of anger. The heat of the blood, or the vital heat of men and of animals in general, proceeds solely from love, which constitutes their life. Neither is infernal fire anything else than love opposed to heavenly love. Thence it is, as was stated above, that the Divine Love appears to the angels in their world as the sun, fiery, like our sun; and that the angels enjoy heat according to their reception of love from Jehovah God by means of that sun.

3   It follows from this that the light there is in its essence wisdom; for love and

wisdom, like Being [*esse*] and Manifestation [*existere*], are indivisible, since love is manifested by means of wisdom and according to it. This is as it is in our world: at the time of spring heat unites itself with light, and causes germination, and at length fruit. Moreover, everyone knows that spiritual heat is love and spiritual light is wisdom; for a man grows warm as he loves, and his understanding is in light as he becomes wise.

I have often seen that spiritual light. It immensely exceeds natural light in brightness and splendour, for it is as brightness and splendour in their very essence: it appears like resplendent and dazzling snow, such as the garments of the Lord appeared when He was transfigured (Mark 9:3; Luke 9:29). As light is wisdom, therefore the Lord calls Himself the light which enlightens every man (John 1:9); and says in other places that He is light itself (John 3:19; 8:12; 12:35, 36, 46); that is, that He is the Divine Truth itself, which is the Word, thus Wisdom itself.

It is believed that natural light [*lumen*], which also is rational, proceeds from the light of our world: but it proceeds from the light of the sun of the spiritual world; for the sight of the mind flows into the sight of the eye, thus also the light of the spiritual world into the light of the natural world, but not the other way round: were it otherwise, there would be physical and not spiritual influx.

Both that heat and that light flow into man:
the heat into his will, where it produces the good of love;
and the light into his understanding, where
it produces the truth of wisdom

7.   I t is well known that all things universally have relation to good and truth, and that there is not a single thing in existence in which there is not something related to those two. On this account there are two receptacles of life in man: one, which is the receptacle of good, called the will; and another, which is the receptacle of truth, called the understanding; and, as good is of love and truth is of wisdom, the will is the receptacle of love, and the understanding the receptacle of wisdom. Good is of love, because what a man loves that he wills, and when he brings it into action he calls it good: and truth is of wisdom, because all wisdom is from truths; indeed, the good which a wise man thinks is truth, which becomes good when he wills and does it.

2   He who does not rightly distinguish between these two receptacles of life, which are the will and the understanding, and does not form for himself a clear notion respecting them, strives in vain to comprehend the nature of spiritual influx. For there is influx into the will, and there is influx into the understanding. Into the will of man there is an influx of the good of love, and into his understanding there is an influx of the truth of wisdom, each proceeding from Jehovah God, directly through the sun in the midst of which He is, and indirectly through the angelic heaven. These two receptacles, the will and the

understanding are as distinct as heat and light; for, as was said above, the will receives the heat of heaven, which in its essence is love, and the understanding receives the light of heaven, which in its essence is wisdom.

There is an influx from the human mind into the speech, and there is an influx into the actions; the influx into speech is from the will through the understanding, but the influx into the actions is from the understanding through the will. Those who are only acquainted with the influx into the understanding, and not at the same time with that into the will, and who reason and conclude therefrom, are like one-eyed persons, who only see the objects on one side of them, and not at the same time those on the other; and like maimed persons, who do their work awkwardly with one hand only; and like lame persons, who walk by hopping on one foot, with the assistance of a staff. From these few observations it is plain that spiritual heat flows into the will of man, and produces the good of love, and that spiritual light flows into his understanding, and produces the truth of wisdom.

3

Those two, heat and light, or love and wisdom,
flow conjointly from God into the soul of man;
and through this into his mind, its affections and thoughts;
and from these into the senses, speech,
and actions of the body

8. The spiritual influx hitherto treated of by inspired men is that from the soul into the body, but no one has treated of influx into the soul, and through this into the body; although it is known that all the good of love and all the truth of faith flow from God into man, and nothing of them from man; and those things which flow from God flow first into his soul, and through his soul into the rational mind, and through this into those things which constitute the body. If any one investigates spiritual influx in any other manner, he is like one who stops up the course of a fountain and still seeks there perennial streams; or like one who deduces the origin of a tree from the root and not from the seed; or like one who examines derivations apart from their source.

2 For the soul is not life in itself, but is a recipient of life from God, who is life in Himself; and all influx is of life, thus from God. This is meant by the statement: *"Jehovah God breathed into man's nostrils the breath of lives, and man was made a living soul"* (Gen. 2:7). To breathe into the nostrils the breath of lives signifies to implant the perception of good and truth. The Lord also says of Himself, *"As the Father hath life in Himself so hath He also given to the Son to have life in Himself"* (John 5:26): life in Himself is God; and the life of the soul is life flowing in from God.

———

Now inasmuch as all influx is of life, and life operates by means of its recep- 3
tacles, and the inmost or first of the receptacles in man is his soul, therefore in
order that influx may be rightly apprehended it is necessary to begin from God,
and not from an intermediate station. Were we to begin from an intermediate
station, our doctrine of influx would be like a chariot without wheels, or like a
ship without sails. This being the case, therefore, in the preceding articles we
have treated of the sun of the spiritual world, in the midst of which is Jehovah
God (no. 5); and of the influx thence of love and wisdom, thus of life (nos. 6, 7).

That life flows from God into man through the soul, and through this into 4
his mind, that is, into its affections and thoughts, and from these into the senses,
speech, and actions of the body, is because these are the things pertaining to life
in successive order. For the mind is subordinate to the soul, and the body is
subordinate to the mind. The mind, also, has two lives, the one of the will and
the other of the understanding. The life of its will is the good of love, the derivations of which are called affections; and the life of the understanding there is
the truth of wisdom, the derivations of which are called thoughts: by means of
the latter and the former the mind lives. The life of the body, on the other hand,
are the senses, speech, and actions: that these are derived from the soul through
the mind follows from the order in which they stand, and from this they mani-
fest themselves to a wise man without examination.

The human soul, being a superior spiritual substance, receives influx 5
directly from God; but the human mind, being an inferior spiritual substance,
receives influx from God indirectly through the spiritual world; and the body,
being composed of the substances of nature which are called matter, receives
influx from God indirectly through the natural world.

That the good of love and the truth of wisdom flow from God into the soul of
a man conjointly, that is, united into one, but that they are divided by the man
in their progress, and are conjoined only with those who suffer themselves to be
led by God, will be seen in the following articles.

———

The sun of the natural world is pure fire; and the world of nature first existed and continually subsists by means of this sun

9. That nature and its world—by which we mean the atmospheres and the earths which are called planets, among which is the terraqueous globe on which we dwell, together with all the productions, in general and in particular, which annually adorn its surface—subsist solely from the sun, which constitutes their centre, and which, by the rays of its light and the modifications of its heat, is everywhere present, everyone knows for certain, from his own experience, from the testimony of the senses, and from the writings which treat of the way in which the world has been peopled. As, therefore, perpetual subsistence is from this source, reason may also conclude with certainty that existence is likewise from the same; for perpetually to subsist is perpetually to exist as a thing first existed. Hence it follows that the natural world was created by Jehovah God by means of this sun as a secondary cause.

2   That there are spiritual things and natural things, entirely distinct from each other, and that the origin and support of spiritual things are from a sun which is pure love, in the midst of which is Jehovah God, the Creator and Upholder of the universe, has been demonstrated before; but that the origin and support of natural things are a sun which is pure fire, and that the latter is derived from the former, and both from God, follows of itself, as what is posterior follows from what is prior, and what is prior from *The First*.

———

That the sun of nature and its worlds is pure fire, all its effects demonstrate: 3
as the concentration of its rays into a focus by the art of optics, from which
proceeds violently burning fire and also flame; the nature of its heat, which is
similar to heat from elementary fire; the graduation of that heat according to
its angle of incidence, whence proceed the varieties of climate, and also the
four seasons of the year; besides many other facts, from which the rational
faculty, by means of the senses of the body, may confirm the truth that the sun
of the natural world is mere fire, and also that it is fire in its utmost purity.

Those who know nothing concerning the origin of spiritual things from   4
their own sun, but are only acquainted with the origin of natural things from
theirs, can scarcely avoid confounding spiritual and natural things together,
and concluding, through the fallacies of the senses and of the rational faculty
derived from them, that spiritual things are nothing but pure natural things,
and that from the activity of these latter, excited by heat and light, arise wisdom
and love. These persons, since they see nothing else with their eyes, and smell
nothing else with their nostrils, and breathe nothing else through their lungs
but nature, ascribe to it all things rational also; and thus they imbibe what is
natural as a sponge sucks up water. Such persons may be compared to chariot-
eers who yoke the team of horses behind the carriage, and not before it.

The case is otherwise with those who distinguish between things spiritual and   5
natural, and deduce the latter from the former. These also perceive the influx of the
soul into the body; they perceive that it is spiritual, and that natural things, which
are those of the body, serve the soul for vehicles and mediums, by which to produce
its effects in the natural world. If you conclude otherwise you may be likened to a
crayfish, which assists its progress in walking with its tail, and draws its eyes back-
ward at every step; and your rational sight may be compared to the sight of the eyes
of Argus in the back of his head, when those in his forehead were asleep. Such
persons also believe themselves to be Arguses in reasoning; for they say, "Who does
not see that the origin of the universe is from nature? And what then is God but the
inmost extension of nature?" and make similar irrational observations, of which
they boast more than wise men do of their rational sentiments.

——

Therefore everything which proceeds from this sun, regarded in itself, is dead

﴾﴿﴾﴿﴾﴿﴾﴿﴾﴿﴾﴿﴾﴿﴾﴿﴾﴿﴾﴿﴾﴿﴾﴿﴾﴿

10. Who does not see from the rational faculty belonging to his understanding, if this be a little elevated above the things of the bodily senses, that love, regarded in itself, is alive, and that the appearance of its fire is life; and, on the contrary, that elementary fire, regarded in itself, is respectively dead; consequently, that the sun of the spiritual world, being pure love, is alive, and that the sun of the natural world, being pure fire, is dead; and that the case is the same with all the products which proceed and exist from them?

2   There are two things which produce all the effects in the universe, *life* and *nature*; and they produce them according to order, when life, from within, actuates nature. The case is otherwise when nature, from within, causes life to act, which occurs with those who place nature, which in itself is dead, above and within life, and thence wholly devote themselves to the pleasures of the senses and the lusts of the flesh, esteeming the spiritual things of the soul, and the truly rational things of the mind, as nothing. These persons, on account of this inversion, are those who are called *the dead*: such are all atheistic materialists in the world, and all the satans in hell.

3   They are also called *the dead* in the Word; as in David: "*They joined themselves also unto Baal-Peor, and ate the sacrifices of the dead*" (Psalm 106:28).

"The enemy persecutes my soul; he makes me to sit in darkness, as the dead of the world" (Psalm 143:3). *"To hear the groaning of the prisoner, and to set at liberty the sons of death"* (Psalm 102:20). And in Revelation: *"I know thy works, that thou hast a name that thou livest, and are dead. Be watchful, and strengthen the things which remain, that are ready to die"* (3:1, 2).

They are called the dead, because spiritual death is condemnation; and condemnation is the lot of those who believe life to be from nature, and thus believe the light of nature to be the light of life, and thereby conceal, suffocate, and extinguish every idea of God, of heaven, and of eternal life. In consequence of so doing, such persons are like owls, which see light in darkness, and darkness in light, that is, they see falsities as truths, and evils as goods, and, as the delights of evil are the delights of their hearts, they are not unlike those birds and beasts which devour dead bodies as choice delicacies, and scent the stenches arising from graves as balsamic odours. They also see no influx but such as is physical or natural; if, notwithstanding, they affirm influx to be spiritual, it is not from any idea of it, but from the mouth of their instructor.

4

That which is spiritual clothes itself with that which is natural, as a man clothes himself with a garment

11. It is well known that both an active and a passive are necessary to every operation, and that nothing can be produced from an active alone, and nothing from a passive alone. It is similar with what is spiritual and what is natural: what is spiritual, as a living force, being active, and what is natural, as a dead force, being passive. Hence it follows that whatever existed in this solar world from the beginning, and whatever comes into existence from moment to moment since, exists from what is spiritual by means of what is natural; and this not only in regard to the subjects of the animal kingdom, but also to those of the vegetable kingdom.

2   Another similar fact is also known, namely, that in every effect which is produced there are both a principal and an instrumental cause, and that these two, when anything is done, appear as one, although they are distinctly two; hence it is one of the laws of wisdom, that the principal cause and the instrumental cause make together one cause; so also do what is spiritual and what is natural. The reason that in producing effects these two appear as one is that the spiritual is within the natural, as a fibre is within a muscle and blood within the arteries, or as thought is inwardly in speech and affection in the tones of the voice; and it causes itself to be felt by means of the natural. From these considerations—though thus far only indistinctly, as through a lattice—it appears

that what is spiritual clothes itself with what is natural, as a man clothes himself with a garment.

The organic body with which the soul clothes itself is here compared with a garment, because it invests the soul; and the soul also withdraws itself from it, and casts it off as old clothing, when it departs by death from the natural into its own spiritual world. Moreover, the body grows old like a garment, but not the soul; because this is a spiritual substance, which has nothing in common with the changes of nature, which advance from their beginnings to their ends, and are terminated at stated times. 3

Those who do not consider the body as a vesture or covering of the soul, which in itself is dead, and only adapted to receive the living forces flowing into it through the soul from God, cannot avoid concluding from fallacies that the soul lives of itself, and the body of itself, and that there is, between their respective lives, a *pre-established harmony*. They likewise infer either that the life of the soul flows into the life of the body, or the life of the body into the life of the soul, whence they conceive *influx* to be either *spiritual* or *natural*: when, nevertheless, it is a truth attested by every object in creation that what is posterior does not act from itself, but from something prior, from which it proceeded; thus that neither does this act from itself, but from something still prior; and thus that nothing acts except from a First, which does act from itself, thus from God. Besides, there is only one life, and this is not capable of being created, but is eminently capable of flowing into forms organically adapted to its reception: all things in the created universe, in general and in particular, are such forms. 4

It is believed by many that the soul is life, and thus that a man, since he lives from his soul, lives from his own life, thus of himself, consequently not by an influx of life from God. But such persons cannot avoid tying a sort of Gordian knot of fallacies, in which they entangle all the judgments of their mind till nothing but insanity in regard to spiritual things is the result; or they construct a maze, from which the mind can never, by any clue of reason, retrace its way and extricate itself. They also actually let themselves down, as it were, into caverns underground, where they dwell in eternal darkness. 5

——

6   For from such a belief proceed innumerable fallacies, each of which is horrible: as that God has transfused and transcribed Himself into men, whence every man is a sort of deity that lives of himself, and thus that he does good and is wise from himself; likewise, that he possesses faith and charity in himself, and thus derives them from himself, and not from God; besides other monstrous sentiments, such as prevail with those in hell, who, when they were in the world, believed nature to live or to produce life by its own activity. When these look towards heaven, its light appears to them as mere thick darkness.

7   I once heard from heaven the voice of some one saying that if a spark of life in man were his own, and not of God in him, there would be no heaven nor anything that exists there; whence also there would be no church on earth, and consequently no life eternal.

For further particulars relating to this subject, the memorable relation in the work on *Conjugial Love*, nos. 132-136,* may be consulted.

---

*See also in *The True Christian Religion*, no. 48.

Spiritual things, thus clothed in a man, enable him to live as a rational and moral man, thus as a spiritually natural man

☯☯☯☯☯☯☯☯☯☯☯☯☯☯☯☯☯

12. **T**his follows as a conclusion from the principle established above, that the soul clothes itself with a body as a man clothes himself with a garment. For the soul flows into the human mind, and through this into the body, bearing with it the life which it continually receives from the Lord, and transferring it thus indirectly into the body, where, by means of the closest union, it causes the body, as it were, to live. From this, and from a thousand testimonies of experience, it is evident that what is spiritual, united to what is material, as a living force with a dead force, causes a man to speak rationally and to act morally.

It appears as if the tongue and lips speak from a certain life in themselves, and as if the arms and hands act in a like manner; but it is the thought, which in itself is spiritual, which speaks, and the will, which is likewise spiritual, which acts, and each by means of its own organs, which in themselves are material, because taken from the natural world. That this is the case appears in the light of day, provided this consideration be attended to: Remove thought from speech, is not the mouth in a moment dumb? So, remove will from action, and do not the hands in a moment become still? 2

The union of spiritual with natural things, and the consequent appearance of life in material objects, may be compared to excellent wine in a clean sponge, 3 to the sweet must in a grape, to the delicious juice in an apple, and to the aromatic odour of cinnamon. The containing fibres of all these are material substances, which of themselves have neither taste nor smell, but derive them from the fluids in and between them; thus, if you squeeze out those juices, they become dead filaments. It is the same with the organs of the body, if life be taken away.

4   That a man is a rational being by virtue of the union of spiritual things with natural is evident from the analytical processes of his thought; and that he is a moral being from the same cause is evident from the excellences of his conduct and the propriety of his demeanour. These he possesses by virtue of his faculty of being able to receive influx from the Lord through the angelic heaven, where there is the very abode of wisdom and love, thus of rationality and morality. Hence it may be perceived that the union in a man of what is spiritual with what is natural causes him to live as a spiritually natural man. The reason that he lives in a similar and yet dissimilar manner after death is that his soul is then clothed in a substantial body, just as in the natural world it was clothed with a material body.

5   It is believed by many that the perceptions and thoughts of the mind, being spiritual, flow in unassisted and not by means of organized forms. Those thus dream, however, who have not seen the interiors of the head, where the perceptions and thoughts are in their beginnings, and who are ignorant that the brains are there, interwoven and composed of the grey and white matter, together with the glands, ventricles, and divisions, and all surrounded by the covering membranes; and who likewise do not know that a man thinks and wills sanely or insanely according to the sound or distorted condition of all those organs; consequently, that he is rational and moral according to the organic structure of his mind. For the rational sight of a man, which is the understanding, without forms organized for the inception of spiritual light, would be an abstract nothing, just as his natural sight would be without eyes; and so in other instances.

XI

The reception of that influx is according to the state of love and wisdom with man

⁜⁜⁜⁜⁜⁜⁜⁜⁜⁜⁜⁜⁜⁜⁜⁜⁜⁜⁜⁜⁜⁜⁜⁜⁜⁜⁜⁜⁜⁜⁜⁜

13. That a man is not life, but an organ recipient of life from God, and that love in union with wisdom is life; also, that God is love itself and wisdom itself, and thus life itself, has been demonstrated above. Hence it follows that so far as a man loves wisdom, or so far as he has wisdom within love, so far he is an image of God, that is, a receptacle of life from God; and on the contrary that so far as he is in the opposite love and thence in insanity, so far he does not receive life from God but from hell, which life is called death.

Love itself and wisdom itself are not life, but are the Being [*esse*] of life. On the other hand, the delights of love and the pleasures of wisdom, which are affections, constitute life; for by their means the Being [*esse*] of life is manifested. The influx of life from God carries with it those delights and pleasures; just as the influx of light and heat in springtime conveys delight and pleasure into human minds, and also into birds and beasts of every kind, and even into vegetables which then put forth their buds and grow fruitful. For the delights of love and the pleasures of wisdom expand the mind and adapt it to reception, just as joy and gladness expand the face and adapt it to the influx of the cheerfulness of the soul.

The man who is affected with the love of wisdom is like the garden in Eden, in which there are two trees, the one of life, and the other of the knowledge of good and evil. The tree of life is the reception of love and wisdom from God, and the tree of the knowledge of good and evil is the reception of them from self. The man who receives them in the latter fashion is insane, yet still believes himself to be wise like God; but he that receives them in the former method is truly wise, and believes no one to be wise but God alone, and that a man is wise so far as he believes this, and still more so as he feels that he wills it. But more on this subject may be seen in the memorable relation inserted in the work on *Conjugial Love*, nos. 132-136.*

4   I will here add an arcanum confirming these facts from heaven. All the angels of heaven turn the front of the head towards the Lord as a sun, and all the angels of hell turn the back of the head to Him. The latter receive influx into the affections of their will, which in themselves are lusts, and make the understanding favour them; but the former receive influx into the affections of their understanding, and make the will favour them; these, therefore, are in wisdom, but the others in insanity. For the human understanding dwells in the cerebrum, which is behind the forehead, and the will in the cerebellum, which is in the back of the head.

5   Who does not know that a man who is insane through falsities favours the lusts of his own evil, and confirms them by reasons drawn from the understanding; whereas a wise man sees from truths the character of the lusts of his own will, and restrains them? A wise man does this, because he turns his face to God, that is, he believes in God, and not in himself; but an insane man does the other, because he turns his face from God, that is, he believes in himself, and not in God. To believe in one's self is to believe that one loves and is wise from self, and not from God, and this is signified by eating of the tree of the knowledge of good and evil; but to believe in God is to believe that one loves and is wise from God and not from self, and this is to eat of the tree of life (Rev. 2:7).

6   From these considerations it may be perceived, but as yet only as in the light

---

*See also *The True Christian Religion*, no. 48.

——

of the moon by night, that the reception of the influx of life from God is according to the state of love and wisdom with a man. This influx may be further illustrated by the influx of light and heat into vegetables, which blossom and bear fruit according to the structure of the fibres which form them, thus according to reception. It may also be illustrated by the influx of the rays of light into precious stones, which modify them into colours according to the arrangement of the parts composing them, thus also according to reception; and likewise by optical glasses and by drops of rain, which exhibit rainbows according to the incidence, the refraction, and thus the reception of light. It is similar with human minds in respect to spiritual light, which proceeds from the Lord as a sun, and perpetually flows in, but is variously received.

The understanding in a man can be raised into the light,
that is, into the wisdom in which are the angels of heaven,
according to the cultivation of his reason; and his will can be
raised in like manner into the heat of heaven, that is, into love,
according to the deeds of his life; but the love of the will is not
raised, except so far as the man wills and does those things
which the wisdom of the understanding teaches

14. By the human mind are to be understood its two faculties, which are called the understanding and the will. The understanding is the receptacle of the light of heaven, which in its essence is wisdom; and the will is the receptacle of the heat of heaven, which in its essence is love, as was shown above. These two, wisdom and love, proceed from the Lord as a sun, and flow into heaven universally and individually, whence the angels have wisdom and love; and they also flow into this world universally and individually, whence men have wisdom and love.

2   Moreover, those two principles proceed in union from the Lord, and likewise flow in union into the souls of angels and men; but they are not received in union in their minds. The first received there is the light which forms the understanding, and by slow degrees the love which forms the will. This also is of Providence: for every man is to be created anew, that is, reformed; and this is effected by means of the understanding. For he must imbibe from infancy the knowledge of truth and good, which will teach him to live well, that is, to will and act rightly: thus the will is formed by means of the understanding.

3   For the sake of this end, there is given to man the faculty of raising his understanding almost into the light in which the angels of heaven are, that he may see what he ought to will and thence to do, in order to be prosperous in the

world for a time, and blessed after death to eternity. He becomes prosperous and blessed if he procures to himself wisdom, and keeps his will in obedience thereto; but unprosperous and unhappy if he puts his understanding under obedience to his will. The reason is that the will inclines from birth towards evils, even to those which are enormous; hence, unless it were restrained by means of the understanding, a man would rush into acts of wickedness, indeed, from his inherent savage nature, he would destroy and slaughter, for the sake of himself, all who do not favour and indulge him.

Besides, unless the understanding could be separately perfected, and the will by means of it, a man would not be a man but a beast. For without that separation, and without the ascent of the understanding above the will, he would not be able to think, and from thought to speak, but only to express his affection by sounds; neither would he be able to act from reason, but only from instinct; still less would he be able to know the things which are of God, and by means of them to know God, and thus to be conjoined to Him, and to live to eternity. For a man thinks and wills *as of himself* and this thinking and willing *as of himself* is the reciprocal element of conjunction: for there can be no conjunction without reciprocity, just as there can be no conjunction of an active with a passive without reaction. God alone acts, and a man suffers himself to be acted upon; and he reacts to all appearance as from himself, though interiorly it is from God. 4

From these considerations, rightly apprehended, may be seen what is the nature of the love of a man's will if it is raised by means of the understanding, and what is its nature if it is not raised; consequently what is the nature of the man. But the nature of a man, if the love of his will is not raised by means of the understanding, shall be illustrated by comparisons. He is like an eagle flying on high, which, as soon as it sees below the food which is the object of its desire, such as chickens, young swans, or even young lambs, casts itself down in a moment and devours them. He is also like an adulterer, who conceals a harlot in a cellar below, and who by turns goes up to the uppermost apartments of the house, and converses wisely with those who dwell there concerning chastity, and 5 from time to time withdraws from the company there and indulges himself below with his harlot.

6   He is also like a thief on a tower, who pretends to keep watch there, but who, as soon as he sees any object of plunder below, hastens down and seizes it. He may also be compared to marsh-flies, which fly in a column over the head of a horse whilst he is running, but which fall down when the horse stops, and plunge into their marsh. Such is the man whose will or love is not raised by means of the understanding; for he then remains below, at the foot, immersed in the unclean things of nature and the lusts of the senses. It is altogether otherwise with those who subdue the allurements of the lusts of the will by means of the wisdom of the understanding. With them the understanding afterwards enters into a marriage covenant with the will, thus wisdom with love, and they dwell together above with the utmost delight.

XIII

It is altogether otherwise with beasts

15. Those who judge from the mere appearance presented to the senses of the body conclude that beasts have will and understanding just in the same manner as men, and hence that the only distinction consists in a man's being able to speak, and thus to utter the things which he thinks and desires, while beasts can only express them by sounds. Beasts, however, have not will and understanding, but only a resemblance of each, which the learned call an analogue.

A man is a man, because his understanding can be raised above the desires of his will, and thus, from above can know and see them, and also govern them; but a beast is a beast, because its desires impel it to do whatever it does. A man is thus a man from the fact that his will is under obedience to his understanding; but a beast is a beast from the circumstance that its understanding is under obedience to its will. From these considerations this conclusion follows: that a man's understanding is alive, and thence a true understanding, because it receives the light flowing in from heaven, and takes possession of it and regards it as its own, and thinks from it analytically with all variety, altogether as if from itself; and that a man's will is alive, and is thence truly will, because it receives the inflowing love of heaven, and acts from it as if from itself; but that the contrary is the case with beasts.

3   Therefore those who think from the lusts of the will are compared to beasts, and likewise, in the spiritual world, appear at a distance as beasts; they also act like beasts, with only this difference, that they are able to act otherwise if they wish. Those, on the other hand, who restrain the lusts of their will by means of the understanding, and thence act rationally and wisely, appear in the spiritual world as men, and are angels of heaven.

4   In a word, the will and the understanding in beasts always work together; and because the will in itself is blind, being a thing of heat and not of light, it makes the understanding blind also. Hence a beast does not know and understand its own actions; yet it acts, notwithstanding, for it acts by an influx from the spiritual world, and such action is instinct.

5   It is supposed that a beast thinks from the understanding what to do; but it does not in the least: it is induced to act solely from the natural love which is in it from creation, with the assistance of the senses of its body. The reason that a man thinks and speaks is simply that his understanding is capable of being separated from his will, and of being raised even into the light of heaven; for the understanding thinks, and the thought speaks.

6   The reason why beasts act according to the laws of order inscribed on their nature, and some of them (differently from many men) in, as it were, a moral and rational manner, is that their understanding is in blind obedience to the desires of their will, and thence they have not been able to pervert those desires by depraved reasonings, as men do. It is to be observed that by the will and understanding of beasts in the foregoing statements we mean a certain resemblance and analogue of those faculties. The analogues are called by the names of those faculties on account of the appearance.

7   The life of a beast may be compared with a sleep-walker, who walks and acts by virtue of the will while the understanding sleeps; and also with a blind man, who passes through the streets with a dog leading him; as likewise with an idiot, who from custom and the habit thence acquired does his work according to rules. It may be similarly compared with a person devoid of memory, and thence deprived of understanding, who still knows or learns how to clothe himself, to

eat the food which he prefers, to love the sex, to walk the streets from house to house, and to do such things as soothe the senses and indulge the flesh, by the allurements and pleasures of which things he is drawn along, though he does not think, and therefore cannot speak.

From these considerations it is evident how much those are mistaken who believe that beasts enjoy rationality, and that they are only distinguished from men by their outward form, and by their inability to express by speech the rational things which they conceal within; from which fallacies many even conclude that if a man lives after death, a beast will live also; and, conversely, that if a beast does not live after death, neither will a man; besides other fancies arising from ignorance in regard to the will and understanding, and also concerning degrees, by means of which, as by a flight of stairs, the mind of a man mounts up to heaven.

XIV

There are three degrees in the spiritual world, and three degrees in the natural world, hitherto unknown, according to which all influx takes place

:❀:❀:❀:❀:❀:❀:❀: ❀:❀: ❀:❀:❀:❀:❀:❀:❀:❀:❀:❀:❀:❀:❀:❀:❀:

16.   It is discovered by the investigation of causes from effects that there are two kinds of degrees: one in which things are prior and posterior, and another in which they are greater and less. The degrees which distinguish things prior and posterior are to be called *degrees of altitude*, or *discrete degrees*; but the degrees by which things greater and less are distinguished from each other are to be called *degrees of latitude*, and also *continuous degrees*.

2   Degrees of altitude, or discrete degrees, are like the generations and compositions of one thing from another; as for example, of some nerve from its fibres, and of any fibre from its fibrils; or of some piece of wood, stone, or metal from its parts, and of any part from its particles. But degrees of latitude, or continuous degrees, are like the increases and decreases of the same degree of altitude with respect to breadth, length, height and depth; as of greater and less volumes of water, air, or ether; and as of large and small masses of wood, stone, or metal.

3   All things in general and in particular in both worlds, the spiritual and the natural, are by creation in degrees of this double kind. The whole animal kingdom in this world is in those degrees, both in general and in particular; so likewise are the whole vegetable kingdom and the whole mineral kingdom; and also the atmospheric expanse from the sun even to the earth.

———

There are, therefore, three atmospheres, discretely distinct according to the degrees of altitude, both in the spiritual and in the natural world, because each world has a sun; but the atmospheres of the spiritual world, by virtue of their origin, are substantial, and the atmospheres of the natural world, by virtue of their origin, are material. Moreover, since the atmospheres descend from their origins according to those degrees, and are the containants of light and heat, and as it were the vehicles by which they are conveyed, it follows that there are three degrees of light and heat; and since the light in the spiritual world is in its essence wisdom, and the heat there in its essence is love, as was shown above in its proper article, it follows also that there are three degrees of wisdom and three degrees of love, consequently three degrees of life; for they are graduated by those things through which they pass. 4

Hence it is that there are three angelic heavens: a supreme, which is also called the third heaven, inhabited by angels of the supreme degree; a middle, which is also called the second heaven, inhabited by angels of the middle degree; and a lowest, which is also called the first heaven, inhabited by angels of the lowest degree. Those heavens are also distinguished according to the degrees of wisdom and love: those who are in the lowest heaven are in the love of knowing truths and goods; those in the middle heaven are in the love of understanding them; and those in the supreme heaven are in the love of being wise, that is, of living according to those truths and goods which they know and understand. 5

As the angelic heavens are distinguished into three degrees, so also is the human mind, because the human mind is an image of heaven, that is, it is heaven in its least form. Hence it is that a man can become an angel of one of those three heavens; and he becomes such according to his reception of wisdom and love from the Lord: an angel of the lowest heaven if he only receives the love of knowing truths and goods; an angel of the middle heaven if he receives the love of understanding them; and an angel of the supreme heaven if he receives the love of being wise, that is, of living according to them. That the human mind is distinguished into three regions, according to the three heavens, may 6 be seen in the memorable relation inserted in the work on *Conjugial Love*, no. 270. Hence it is evident that all spiritual influx to a man and into a man from the Lord descends through these three degrees, and that it is received by the man according to the degree of wisdom and love in which he is.

7   A knowledge of these degrees is, at the present day, of the greatest value: for many persons, in consequence of not knowing them, remain in and cling to the lowest degree, in which are the senses of their body; and from their ignorance, which is a thick darkness of the understanding, they cannot be raised into spiritual light, which is above them. Hence naturalism takes possession of them, as it were spontaneously, as soon as they attempt to enter on any enquiry and examination concerning the soul and the human mind and its rationality; and still more if they extend their inquiries to heaven and the life after death. Hence they become like persons standing in the market-places with telescopes in their hands, looking at the sky and uttering vain predictions; and also like persons who chatter and reason about every object they see and everything they hear, without anything rational from the understanding being contained in their remarks; but they are like butchers, who believe themselves to be skilful anatomists, because they have examined the viscera of oxen and sheep outwardly, but not inwardly.

8   The truth, however, is, that to think from the influx of natural light [*lumen*] not enlightened by the influx of spiritual light is merely to dream, and to speak from such thought is to make vain assertions like fortune-tellers. But further particulars concerning degrees may be seen in the work on *The Divine Love and Wisdom*, nos. 173-281.

XV

Ends are in the first degree, causes in the second, and effects in the third

17. Who does not see that the end is not the cause, but that it produces the cause, and that the cause is not the effect, but that it produces the effect, consequently, that these are three distinct things which follow one another in order? The end with a man is the love of his will; for what a man loves, this he proposes to himself and intends: the cause with him is the reason of his understanding; for by means of reason the end seeks for middle or efficient causes: and the effect is the operation of the body, from and according to the end and the cause. Thus there are three things in a man which follow one another in order, in the same manner as the degrees of altitude follow one another. When these three are established, the end is inwardly in the cause, and, by means of the cause, the end is in the effect: thus these three exist together in the effect. On this account it is said in the Word that every one shall be judged according to his works; for the end, or the love of his will, and the cause, or the reason of his understanding, are simultaneously present in the effects, which are the works of his body: thus in them is contained the quality of the whole man.

Those who do not know these truths, and thus do not distinguish the objects of reason, cannot avoid terminating the ideas of their thought either in the

2

atoms of Epicurus, the monads of Leibnitz, or the simple substances of Wolff. Inevitably, therefore, they shut up the understanding as with a bolt, so that it cannot even think from reason concerning spiritual influx, because it cannot think of any progression; for, says the author concerning his simple substance, if it is divided it falls to nothing. Thus the understanding remains in its own first light [*lumen*], which merely proceeds from the senses of the body, and does not advance a step further. Hence it is not known but that the spiritual is the natural attenuated; that beasts have rationality as well as men; and that the soul is a puff of wind, like that breathed forth from the chest when a person dies; besides several ideas which are not of the light, but of thick darkness.

3   As all things in the spiritual world, and all things in the natural world, proceed according to these degrees, as was shown in the preceding article, it is evident that intelligence properly consists in knowing and distinguishing them, and seeing them in their order. By means of these degrees, also, every man is known as to his quality, when his love is known; for, as observed above, the end which is of the will, the causes which are of the understanding, and the effects which are of the body follow from his love, as a tree from its seed, and as fruit from a tree.

4   There are three kinds of loves: the love of heaven, the love of the world, and the love of self; the love of heaven is spiritual, the love of the world material, and the love of self corporeal. When the love is spiritual, all the things which follow from it, as forms from their essence, derive a spiritual quality: so, also, if the principal love is the love of the world or of wealth, and thus material, all the things which follow from it, as derivatives from their first origin, derive a material quality: so, again, if the principal love is the love of self, or of eminence above all others, and thus corporeal, all the things which follow from it derive a corporeal quality; because the man who cherishes this love regards himself alone, and thus immerses the thoughts of his mind in the body. Therefore, as just remarked, he who knows the reigning love of any one, and is at the same time acquainted with the progression of ends to causes and of causes to effects, which three things follow one another in order according to the degrees of

altitude, knows the whole man. In this way the angels of heaven know every one with whom they speak: they perceive his love from the sound of his voice; from his face they see an image of him; and from the gestures of his body his character.

XVI

Hence it is evident what is the nature of spiritual influx from its origin to its effects

❦❦❦❦❦❦❦❦❦❦❦❦❦❦❦❦❦❦❦❦

18.   Spiritual influx has hitherto been deduced from the soul into the body, but not from God into the soul and thus into the body. This has been done because no one had any knowledge concerning the spiritual world and the sun there from which all spiritual things stream forth as from their fountain: and thus no one had any knowledge concerning the influx of spiritual things into natural.

2   Now, since it has been granted me to be in the spiritual world and in the natural world at the same time, and thus to see each world and each sun, I am obliged by my conscience to communicate these things. For of what use is knowledge unless it be communicated? What is it, but like collecting and storing up riches in a casket, and only looking at them occasionally and counting them over, without any intention of applying them to use? Spiritual avarice is nothing else.

3   But in order that it may be fully known what spiritual influx is, and what is its nature, it is necessary to know what that which is *spiritual* is in its essence, and what that which is *natural*; and also what the *human soul* is: lest, therefore, this short treatise should be defective through ignorance of these subjects, it will be useful to consult some memorable relations inserted in the work on *Conjugial Love*: concerning what is *spiritual*, in the memorable relation there,

nos. 326-329; concerning the *human soul*, no. 315; and concerning the *influx of spiritual things into natural*, at no. 380; and more fully at nos. 415-422.*

19. To these observations I will add this *memorable relation*. After these pages were written, I prayed to the Lord that I might be permitted to converse with some disciples of Aristotle, and at the same time with some disciples of Descartes, and with some disciples of Leibnitz, in order that I might learn the opinions of their minds concerning the interaction of the soul and the body. After my prayer was ended there came nine men——three Aristotelians, three Cartesians, and three Leibnitzians——and stood around me; the admirers of Aristotle being on the left side, the followers of Descartes on the right, and the favourers of Leibnitz behind. At a considerable distance, and also at a distance from one another, I saw three persons crowned, as it were, with laurel, whom I knew, by an inflowing perception, to be those three great leaders or masters themselves. Behind Leibnitz stood a person holding the skirt of his garment, who, I was told, was Wolff. Those nine men, when they beheld one another, at first saluted one another with courteous speech, and talked together.

But presently there arose from below a spirit with a torch in his right hand, which he shook before their faces, whereupon they became enemies, three against three, and looked fiercely at one another, for they were seized with the lust of altercation and dispute. Then the Aristotelians, who were also Schoolmen, began to speak, saying, "Who does not see that objects flow through the senses into the soul, as a man enters through the doors into a chamber, and that the soul thinks according to such influx? When a lover sees a beautiful virgin, or his bride, does not his eye sparkle, and transmit the love of her into the soul? When a miser sees bags of money, does he not burn towards them with every sense, and thence cause this ardour to enter the soul, and excite the desire of possessing them? When a proud man hears himself praised by another, does he not prick up his ears, and do not these transmit those praises to the soul? Are

2

---

* The same articles may be found in *The True Christian Religion*, at nos. 280, 697, 35, 77 and 12.

not the senses of the body like outer courts, through which alone entrance is obtained to the soul? From these considerations and innumerable others of similar nature, who can conclude otherwise than that influx proceeds from nature, or is physical?"

3   While they were speaking thus, the followers of Descartes held their fingers on their foreheads; and now withdrawing them they replied, saying, "Ah, you speak from appearances. Do you not know that the eye does not love a virgin or bride from itself, but from the soul; and likewise that the senses of the body do not covet the bags of money from themselves, but from the soul; and also that the ears do not devour the praises of flatterers in any other manner? Is it not perception that causes sensation? And perception is of the soul, and not of the bodily organ. Say, if you can, what causes the tongue and lips to speak, but the thought; and what causes the hands to work, but the will? And thought and will are of the soul, and not of the body. Thus, what causes the eye to see, and the ears to hear, and the other organs to feel, but the soul? From these considerations, and innumerable others of a similar kind, everyone, whose wisdom rises above the things of the bodily senses, concludes that there is no influx of the body into the soul, but of the soul into the body; which influx we call Occasional, and also Spiritual Influx."

4   When these had been heard, the three men who stood behind the former groups of three, and who were the favourers of Leibnitz, began to speak, saying, "We have heard the arguments on both sides, and have compared them; and we have perceived that in many particulars the latter are stronger than the former, and that in many others the former are stronger than the latter; wherefore, if you please, we will adjust the dispute." On being asked, "How?" they replied, "There is not any influx of the soul into the body, nor of the body into the soul; but there is a unanimous and instantaneous operation of both together, to which a celebrated author has assigned an elegant name, by calling it Pre-established Harmony."

5   After this the spirit with a torch appeared again. Now, however, the torch was in his left hand, and he shook it behind their heads; whence the ideas of them

all became confused, and they cried out at once, "Neither our soul nor our body knows which side we should take: wherefore let us settle this dispute by lot, and we will abide by the lot which comes out first." So they took three pieces of paper, and wrote on one of them, *physical influx*, on another, *spiritual influx*, and on the third, *pre-established harmony*; and they put them all into the crown of a hat. They then chose one of their number to draw, who, on putting in his hand, took out that on which was written *spiritual influx*. Having seen and read it, they all said——some with a clear and flowing, some with a faint and indrawn voice——"Let us abide by this, because it came out first."

But then an angel suddenly stood by and said, "Do not imagine that the paper in favour of Spiritual Influx came out first by chance, for it was of Providence. Because you are in confused ideas, you do not see its truth; but the very truth presented itself to the hand of him that drew the lots, that you might yield it your assent."

6

20. I was once asked how, from a philosopher, I became a theologian; and I answered, "In the same manner that fishermen were made disciples and apostles by the Lord: and that I also had from early youth been a spiritual fisherman." On this, my questioner asked, "What is a spiritual fisherman?" I replied, "A fisherman, in the Word, in its spiritual sense, signifies a man who investigates and teaches natural truths, and afterwards spiritual truths, in a rational manner."

On his inquiring, "How is this demonstrated?" I said, "From these passages of the Word: *'Then the waters shall fail from the sea, and the river shall be wasted and dried up. Therefore the fishers shall mourn, and all they that cast a hook into the sea shall be sad"* (Isa. 19:5, 8). In another place it is said: *'On the river, the waters whereof were healed, stood fishers from Engedi; they were present at the spreading forth of nets; their fish was according to its kinds, as the fish of the great sea, exceeding many'* (Ezek. 47:10). And in another place: *'Behold I will send for many fishers, saith Jehovah, and they shall fish the sons of Israel* (Jer. 16:16). Hence it is evident why the Lord chose fishermen for His disciples,

2

and said *'Follow Me, and I will make you fishers of men'* (Matt. 4:18, 19; Mark 1:16, 17): and why He said to Peter, after he had caught the multitude of fishes, *'Henceforth thou shalt catch men'* (Luke 5:9, 10).''

3   I afterwards demonstrated the origin of this signification of fishermen from *The Apocalypse Revealed*: namely, that since water signifies natural truths (nos. 50, 932), as does also a river (nos. 409, 932), a fish signifies those who are in natural truths (no. 405); and thence that fishermen signify those who investigate and teach truths.

4   On hearing this, my questioner raised his voice and said, "Now I can understand why the Lord called and chose fishermen to be His disciples; and therefore I do not wonder that He has also chosen you, since, as you have observed, you were from early youth a fisherman in a spiritual sense, that is, an investigator of natural truths: and the reason that you are now become an investigator of spiritual truths is because these are founded on the former." To this he added, being a man of reason, that "the Lord alone knows who is the proper person to apprehend and teach those things which belong to His New Church; whether one of the Primates, or one of their domestic servants." "Besides," he continued, "what Christian theologian does not study philosophy in the schools, before he graduates as a theologian? From what other source has he intelligence?"

5   At length he said, "Since you are become a theologian, explain what is your theology?" I answered, "These are its two principles, *there is one God*, and *there is a conjunction of charity and faith*." To which he replied, "Who denies these principles?" I rejoined, "The theology of the present day, when interiorly examined."

Index